RT GRIFFIN III

BY WILL GRAVES

Published by ABDO Publishing Company, PO Box 398166, Minneapolis, MN 55439.
Copyright © 2014 by Abdo Consulting Group, Inc. International copyrights reserved in all countries. No part of this book may be reproduced in any form without written permission from the publisher. SportsZone™ is a trademark and logo of ABDO Publishing Company.

Printed in the United States of America,
North Mankato, Minnesota
052013
092013

Editor: Chrös McDougall
Series Designer: Craig Hinton

Photo Credits: Paul Abell/AP Images, cover, 1; Aaron M. Sprecher/AP Images, 4, 7; Mary Altaffer/AP Images, 8; Steve Traynor/AP Images, 11; Tony Gutierrez/AP Images, 12, 14, 17; Cal Sport Media via AP Images, 18; Dave Martin/AP Images, 20; Jason DeCrow/AP Images, 23; Tom Gannam/AP Images, 24; Pablo Martinez Monsivais/AP Images, 27; Matt Slocum/AP Images, 28

Library of Congress Control Number: 2013934740

Cataloging-in-Publication Data
Graves, Will.
 Robert Griffin III: RGIII - NFL sensation / Will Graves.
   p. cm. -- (Playmakers)
ISBN 978-1-61783-700-5
1. Griffin, Robert, III, 1990- --Juvenile literature. 2. Football players--United States--Biography--Juvenile literature. 3. Quarterbacks (Football)--United States--Biography--Juvenile literature.   I. Title.
796.332092--dc23
[B]   2013934740

TABLE OF CONTENTS

Robert Griffin III

CHAPTER 1

A SPECIAL TALENT

Robert Griffin III looked across the line of scrimmage. He took a deep breath and waited for the snap. It was 2012. Robert was a rookie quarterback for the Washington Redskins. His National Football League (NFL) career was just a few minutes old. But he was facing his first big test. The Redskins were backed up near their end zone. Robert—whose nickname is RG3—could see the New Orleans Saints getting ready to blitz.

Washington Redskins quarterback Robert Griffin III runs with the ball against the New Orleans Saints in 2012.

Robert took the snap. He waited a couple of seconds for his wide receivers to get open. Finally he threw a laser to wide receiver Pierre Garcon. Robert was knocked to the ground on the play. But Garcon caught the ball and raced 88 yards for a touchdown.

The Redskins ended up winning the game 40–32. Washington later went on to win its division for the first time in 13 years. And it all started with that first big moment. That is when Robert proved he was ready to be an NFL superstar. Maybe no one should have doubted him.

Not many NFL players were born in Japan. Then again, there are not a lot of people quite like Robert—in football or in life. His parents, Robert Jr. and Jacqueline, both worked in the Army. They lived all over the world. So Robert was born on

Robert set two NFL rookie records in 2012. He had the best quarterback rating ever for a rookie at 102.4. Quarterback rating is a complicated measurement of a quarterback's overall performance. And he threw just five interceptions in 393 passes, which also was a record.

Griffin celebrates after throwing a touchdown pass against the New Orleans Saints in his 2012 NFL debut.

February 12, 1990, in Okinawa, Japan. But the family did not stay there long. Robert, his parents, and his two older sisters moved four times when he was young. They finally settled in Fort Hood, Texas, when Robert was seven years old.

It was in Texas that Robert finally found his way to football. However, his parents only let him play if he did his schoolwork

Griffin's dad, *right*, joined him for a press conference after the 2012 NFL Draft.

first. Those were the rules. Robert had to complete all of his homework and earn good grades. Then he could play ball and also earn extra allowance.

The Griffins put down roots in Texas. But Robert's dad still had to travel for the Army. On Robert's thirteenth birthday, in 2003, his father learned he was going to Kuwait the next morning. The US Army sent troops to that country to help in the war in Iraq. Robert's dad asked him to look out for his mother and his sisters while he was away.

Robert Jr. returned home at the end of 2003. He retired from the Army after that and took on a new role as Robert's coach. Robert's talent as a football player was well known by his senior year at Copperas Cove High School. He was stronger and faster than most players. That made it hard for opponents to tackle him. Plus Robert could also beat opposing defenses with his great passing arm.

Robert led Copperas Cove to the state title game as a senior in 2007. The team lost in the championship game by less than a touchdown. He hardly had time to dwell on the loss,

In addition to football, Robert was also a high school track-and-field star. He set Texas high school records in the 110-meter hurdles and the 300-meter hurdles. And he ran so fast in the 400-meter hurdles that he qualified for the 2008 US Olympic Trials. Robert made it all the way to the semifinals before missing the cut.

though. Robert's hard work and good grades allowed him to graduate from high school a semester early.

A lot of colleges wanted Robert to come and play football for their teams. But not all of the coaches were convinced that Robert would be a good college quarterback. Some coaches thought his speed would make him better suited to play a position such as wide receiver or running back.

In the end, only one school offered Robert a chance to play quarterback and run track: Baylor University. Football coach Art Briles had just been hired to turn the Bears into winners. Robert jumped at the chance to make a difference at Baylor. Besides, it was just a little more than an hour from his home, and his older sister was already in school there.

Robert was a good student, a star athlete, and a popular classmate. In fact, Robert was voted class president during his senior year at Copperas Cove High School.

Griffin, *right*, the Copperas Cove quarterback, follows his running back during the Texas championship game in 2007.

Just like always, Robert was prepared. His father says Robert went to college with a plan. Robert ended up pulling it off to perfection.

Robert Griffin III

CHAPTER 2

FULFILLING A PROMISE

Before Griffin even stepped on campus at Baylor, he had a goal. Only his goal was not about doing something on the football field or on the track. It was more difficult than that.

Griffin told his older sister DeJon that he would finish college before she did. He did not care that DeJon had more than a year head start. That is because if there is anything Griffin likes more than football, it is a challenge.

Griffin looks for a receiver during a 2010 Baylor game against Texas Christian University.

Griffin hands off to Baylor running back Jay Finley during a 2008 home game against the University of Oklahoma.

Things took some time to come together in football. Griffin made a splash as a freshman in 2008. He became the starting quarterback in the second game of the season. He passed for more than 2,000 yards and 15 touchdowns that year. But his quarterback skills could not help the defense. The Bears often lost games even though Griffin played very well.

Baylor ended up winning just four games that season. Still, Griffin won a bunch of awards for his outstanding play. Griffin expected to take the next step in 2009. And he got off to a good start. Then his career changed forever against Northwestern State University in the third game of the season. Griffin hurt his right knee. He tried to stay on the field, but the pain was too severe.

Griffin was forced to have surgery to repair his knee. He missed the rest of the season as once again the Bears won just four games. Griffin was able to take a redshirt season.

Griffin could not play football for months while he let his knee heal. That did not stop him from excelling in the classroom or helping others in his community, though. He worked as a volunteer track coach at Baylor while he got better. He went to local high schools to talk to athletes who were also trying to

College athletes are very busy. Two-sport college athletes are even busier. Yet Griffin still took more classes than most regular students. And the heavy workload did not hurt his grades. He ended up making the dean's list twice.

deal with injuries. Griffin volunteered with the Special Olympics as well. And he visited young students who were having a hard time staying out of trouble.

After missing almost a year, Griffin returned to football in 2010. With their leader back on the field, the Bears finally became winners. Baylor went 7–6 that year. And it made it to a bowl game for the first time since 1994.

The Bears succeeded behind Griffin. He passed for 3,501 yards and 22 touchdowns that season. He also set 11 school records. The other coaches in the Big 12 Conference named him the Comeback Player of the Year. That award goes to a player who had to overcome something such as an injury to get back on the field.

Griffin was even better as a junior in 2011. He helped the Bears have one of their best seasons ever. Baylor started

Griffin earned his bachelor's degree in political science in 2010. He spent his final year at Baylor working on his master's degree in communications.

Griffin (10) and his Baylor teammates celebrate after beating Stephen F. Austin State University in 2011.

the season by beating powerful Texas Christian University in an upset. Griffin was spectacular that game, throwing for five touchdowns.

Griffin's great play started to earn him special attention. Still, he made sure to pass on the praise to his teammates. He wanted to make sure everyone knew Baylor's success was a team effort.

Griffin sets up to throw a pass against the Iowa State University Cyclones in 2011.

The wins kept piling up. Griffin became one of the most famous athletes in the country. Always wearing a smile, Griffin treated everyone the same, whether it was another player, a fan, or a classmate.

By the end of the season, Griffin had led Baylor to a 10–3 record. The Bears' 10 wins tied for the most in school history. And that was not the only history the Bears made that season. Griffin won the Heisman Trophy for being the best player in college football. He was the first player from Baylor to win the award. He thanked everyone from his parents to his coaches to God during his acceptance speech. Griffin said winning the award was "unbelievably believable."

By the end of 2011, Griffin had graduated from college and helped make the Baylor football team a winner, just like he had promised. He could have returned to the football team for one more year. But Griffin thought he had already done all he could. He had his degree. He had the Heisman Trophy. Next stop, the NFL.

"The way I looked at it was that not everybody gets an opportunity to say they graduated in three years from college. I said, if I have an opportunity to do it, why not go for it." —Robert Griffin III

Robert Griffin III

CHAPTER 3

PREPPING FOR THE PROS

Every spring after the NFL season ends, the focus turns to the NFL Draft. After winning the Heisman Trophy, Griffin knew he was among the best. So did every team in the NFL.

The Indianapolis Colts had the first pick in the draft. They needed a quarterback after cutting superstar Peyton Manning. The Washington Redskins needed a quarterback, too. So they traded for the second pick in the draft.

Griffin leaps into the air to warm up before running a 40-yard dash at the 2012 NFL combine.

By then, everyone knew Griffin and former Stanford University quarterback Andrew Luck would be the first two picks. But who would go first?

The two players had little in common. Luck was tall and strong. He played like a guy who had been in the NFL for years and years. Griffin was smaller and faster. He did not really play like anybody the NFL had ever seen.

The draft is a big deal to NFL teams. They spend a lot of money on the players they select. So the NFL brings in the top college players to an event called a combine, where teams can evaluate them before the draft.

One of the tests at the combine is a 40-yard dash. That helps teams get a feel for how quick a player is. Griffin's time was 4.41 seconds. It was one of the fastest times ever by a

Griffin is not just fast. He can jump, too. Players do a vertical jump test at the combine. That is when they jump straight up as high as they can. Griffin recorded a vertical jump of 39 inches (0.99 m) at the draft combine. That is more than three feet!

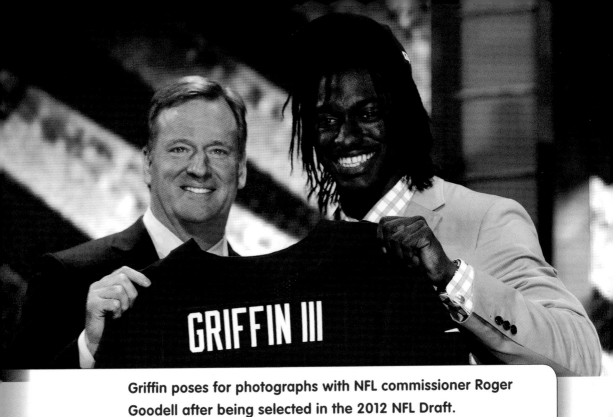

Griffin poses for photographs with NFL commissioner Roger Goodell after being selected in the 2012 NFL Draft.

quarterback. He proved that he was more than just a runner, though. His passes were right on target, too.

The Colts decided to go with Luck. That was fine by Griffin, though. He indeed went second to the Redskins. Griffin walked onto the stage with a big smile. As he pulled on a Redskins hat, he also pulled up the leg of his pants. He was wearing burgundy and gold socks. Those are the colors of the Redskins' jerseys. Griffin was ready to take both the nation's capital and professional football by storm.

Robert Griffin III

CHAPTER 4

MAKING AN IMPACT

G riffin's arrival in Washington gave the Redskins a jolt. His No. 10 jersey became one of the most popular among the league's fans right away. Redskins coach Mike Shanahan named Griffin the starter just a couple of weeks after the draft. The only question now was how would the Redskins use him?

The Redskins knew they needed to take advantage of Griffin's speed. Speed has its drawbacks,

Griffin and Washington Redskins coach Mike Shanahan talk before a 2012 game against St. Louis.

though. A quarterback who runs a lot also gets tackled a lot. That makes him more likely to get injured than a quarterback who mostly hands off or passes the ball.

Sometimes NFL coaches try to teach fast quarterbacks to stay in the pocket. But Shanahan decided it was the Redskins who needed to change. Shanahan said Griffin would let the Redskins do some things that had never been done before in the NFL. So Shanahan watched a lot of tape of Griffin playing at Baylor. In the end, the Redskins borrowed a lot of the plays Griffin had run with the Bears.

Most quarterbacks line up under the center before each play. The Redskins let Griffin work out of the shotgun. That meant he stood a few feet behind the center and had the ball snapped to him. By doing that, Griffin had more freedom to decide whether to run or pass on a play.

"One thing the NFL is not used to is a quarterback with his type of speed and his type of throwing ability. So I think we can do some things that people haven't done." —Redskins coach Mike Shanahan on Griffin

Griffin runs away from a Minnesota Vikings defender during a Redskins victory in 2012.

Griffin's first regular-season game was on the road against the tough New Orleans Saints. Yet he passed for 320 yards and two touchdowns. He also ran nine times for 42 yards. The Redskins surprised many by winning 40–32.

The Redskins struggled after that. They were just 3–6 after nine games. But Griffin was playing like a superstar. Every week

Griffin runs onto the field before the Redskins' January 2013 playoff game against the Seattle Seahawks.

he seemed to make at least one spectacular play. Against the Minnesota Vikings it was 76-yard touchdown run. That was the longest ever by a Washington quarterback. Against the Dallas Cowboys on Thanksgiving, he passed for four touchdowns.

And after the bye week the Redskins got hot, too. They won their final seven games to finish with a 10–6 record. That meant they were going to the playoffs for the first time in five years.

Griffin certainly won over folks who thought he wouldn't make it in the NFL. He passed for 3,200 yards and 20 touchdowns. Plus he ran for 815 yards and seven scores.

After the season he beat out Andrew Luck to be named the NFL's Offensive Rookie of the Year.

It was not easy, though. Griffin injured his right knee late in the season. It was the same knee he hurt when he was at Baylor. Griffin tried to be tough and play through it against the Seattle Seahawks in the playoffs. He limped at times. But he still led the Redskins to a quick 14–0 lead over Seattle.

Unfortunately, it did not last. Griffin took a bad step while dropping back to pass in the third quarter. He fell to the ground, clutching his knee. His season was over. Washington's was too after a 24–14 loss. A few days later, Griffin had surgery on his right knee. It was a disappointing end to a great rookie season. But Redskins fans were happy to finally have another quarterback who could lead the team into the playoffs.

Washington Redskins fans were eager to have a star to cheer for. So when the team drafted Griffin, fans bought Griffin jerseys. And they bought a lot of them. Griffin's No. 10 Redskins jersey was the NFL's highest seller from April 2012 to March 2013. In fact, no jersey in NFL history had sold as much as Griffin's in a single year.

FUN FACTS AND QUOTES

- "The only thing Robert did was homework and play ball. He was very grounded, very rooted." —Copperas Cove High School football coach Jack Welch on Robert Griffin III

- "He'll cause some sleepless nights for [an opposing] coach." —University of Nebraska coach Bo Pellini on Griffin

- How fast was Griffin on the track? When he ran the 300-meter hurdles in high school, his best time was 35.33 seconds. That was just .01 seconds off the record for the fastest time ever by a high school athlete.

- Griffin has always loved funky socks. Sometimes when he played at Baylor, he would wear socks that looked like the ones from Superman's costume. He also has Cookie Monster, SpongeBob SquarePants, and Elmo socks.

- After Griffin graduated from Baylor, the school decided to honor him by creating the "RG3 Scholarship." The scholarship will be given to Baylor's top quarterback every year to help pay for school and books.

WEB LINKS

To learn more about Robert Griffin III, visit ABDO Publishing Company online at **www.abdopublishing.com**. Web sites about Griffin are featured on our Book Links page. These links are routinely monitored and updated to provide the most current information available.

GLOSSARY

bowl game
An extra game winning college football teams play at the end of the season. The games are usually played in late December or January.

combine
An event at which NFL teams evaluate top college players who will be available in the upcoming draft.

dean's list
A list of the students with the best grades at a college or university.

draft
An annual event during which NFL teams select the top college football players.

interception
In football, a pass thrown to a teammate but caught by someone on the opposing team.

playoffs
A series of games played after the regular season to determine which teams go on to the Super Bowl.

pocket
An area behind the line of scrimmage and between the two offensive tackles.

redshirt
A season during which a college athlete sits out to gain experience without losing a year of eligibility.

rookie
A first-year player in the NFL.

scholarship
Financial assistance awarded to students to help them pay for college. Top athletes earn scholarships to represent a college through its sports teams.

INDEX

FURTHER RESOURCES

Basen, Ryan. *Washington Redskins*. Edina, MN: ABDO Publishing Co., 2011.

Hoblin, Paul. *Andrew Luck: Rising NFL Star*. Minneapolis, MN: ABDO Publishing
    Co., 2013.

Wilner, Barry. *The Super Bowl*. Minneapolis, MN: ABDO Publishing Co., 2013.